P9-CAM-589

Women's Poetry: Poems and Advice

PITT POETRY SERIES

Ed Ochester, Editor

Women's Poetry

POEMS AND ADVICE

Daisy Fried

UNIVERSITY OF PITTSBURGH PRESS

Published by the University of Pittsburgh Press, Pittsburgh, Pa., 15260
Copyright © 2013, Daisy Fried
All rights reserved
Manufactured in the United States of America
Printed on acid-free paper
10 9 8 7 6 5 4 3 2 1
ISBN 13: 978-0-8229-6238-0
ISBN 10: 0-8229-6238-1

for Jim and Maisie

CONTENTS

I

II

III

Attenti Agli Zingari

IV

Women's Poetry: Poems and Advice

I

Torment

"I fucked up bad": Justin cracks his neck,
talking to nobody. Fifteen responsible children,
final semester college seniors, bloodshot,
collars undone, gorgeously exhausted,
return from Wall Street interviews
in attitudes of surrender on the Dinky—
the one-car commuter train connecting
Princeton to the New York line. Panic-sweat
sheens their faces. Justin hasn't seen me yet.
"Something's fucked with my tie." He's right.
I see his future, the weight he'll gain
first in his face, then gut and ass, the look
of bad luck he'll haunt his bad jobs with.
He tears off the tie. Elephants on it.

Fatigue, swollen ankles, the midwife said.
The worst discomforts of pregnancy.
I wrote those down. But she's wrong:
self-pity. *Strange dreams,* she said.
No dreams. Discarded newspapers—
business section, money, real estate, auto—
sift apart to quartos and folios underfoot.
"Shut up, Justin," says the girl across from him.
I hardly recognize Brianna in her interview hair.
She scratches her face, fingers trembling
from the day's aftershocks. "I wanted,"
she counts on her fingers, performing
the sitcom of her tragedy, "Tribeca loft,
expense account, designer clothes so haute
they don't look it, my very own Tesla, summer
home in the Hamptons I'm too busy to use."
"You wanted money," says Justin.
Brianna: "It went down with the towers."

I spent my lopsided day lifting my belly
back towards center, interviewing for adjunct jobs.
There's a half-moon in half-clouds
up over the tracks. Justin spreads
over three seats, texts with his thumbs,
talks: "The Lehman Brothers guy asks me,
Did you ever sell anything? Sell me a bottle of water.
I'm like fu-uck. To say something I say
'Why do you like water?' He says . . . "
Justin fixes a diamond stud back in his ear.
"They'll let me know." Fifteen responsible children
sigh in disappointed relief. Somebody they know
didn't get the job they didn't get. I sleep. Wake.
Beautiful clothes spread bodiless before me!
Tailored black suits and skirts, silk ties,
ephemera of sheer and filmy stockings
deflated over seat backs. Brianna looks around,
no conductor coming, squats to peel off,
in one motion, skirt, hose, underpants, step
butt-naked into soft chino shorts I'll never
be able to afford. "Nervous crotch sweat," she says.

I keep trying to look not-quite-40
in a different way than I'm not-quite-40.
The woman interviewer looked at my belly.
"As a new mother would you have time to be
literary mama to your students?" So I could sue
when they don't hire me for the job I don't want.
Justin looks up from his iPhone: "Soon-Ji
got three offers. Fuck." He flips the curl
his mother's fingers crimped, first day of pre-K
into his four-year-old forelock. "He's guessing
he'll go with Goldman Sachs." Brianna grabs her neck
in living garrote. She high-fives anybody

she can reach in gloomy delight. She gobbles
snack-pack popcorn, licks her fingers; bits drop
yellow from her lips. "My mom will go crazy
Deutsche Bank didn't offer." She sees me.
"I didn't realize that was you with your hair up.
Look, Just." She high-fives me. "It's Professor."

Is Brianna crying? "Don't call me Professor,"
I say, dozens of times a semester. "I'm a writer,
not a teacher." Justin grabs a *Norton Anthology*
out of his five-hundred-dollar briefcase. "Fuck.
What are we supposed to read for tomorrow?"
"Prufrock, dummy," Brianna says. "You're
a good professor." She condescends through tears.
"Poor baby," mocks Justin, slumping so low
in the seat I only see his shoe soles on the armrest.
The train swooshes through suburban tracts.
The moon gets smaller. Brianna arrives
mornings to workshop in a fake hurry
and the sweats she slept in, probably rolls back
in bed after. She hands out slight, surprising poems,
apologizes, sips cardboard-container coffee
in a recyclable sleeve, turns her BlackBerry to vibrate.
It moans like indigestion through class.

I hand her one of my self-pity tissues. My ankles
are slim. Brianna hates her name. "So tacky.
I'd be a Kelly if I were twenty years older."
I'd like to be able to hate her. I'm turning
into my Favorite Teachers—so kind,
so industrious, so interested and interesting.
"Sorry I'm late with my portfolio," she says
through sniffles. She dabs her lip. "I had to prepare for,"
a breath, "interviews." A few times a semester

I say, "It's only poetry." *Gumbleeds! nosebleeds!*
the midwife predicted, and it's true, my Kleenexes
are measled with blood, *weird hairs, stretch marks,*
frequent catnaps, hip joints so loose you must
take care walking. The fetus dabs its fingers
in the sponge of me, flails. At the second class,
Brianna said, "My mom would go crazy.
I can't read all these sex poems. We're Christian."
I said, "Poems should be about life,
part of life is sex." Two kids wrote that down
in notebooks. One was Justin. "But skip
any reading that makes you uncomfortable."
Next week, Brianna wrote about hanging
onto stall walls in her residence hall bathroom,
fucking Princeton boys one by one.
Justin's poem was "Torment," seven pages long.

Favorite teachers write poems about students!
Reading them is like listening to whores
talk about clients; however contemptuous they sound,
everybody knows who's selling, who's buying.
I'd like to be able to like them. I sleep. Wake.
"Justin's your boyfriend?" I whisper to Brianna.
My cell phone rings, screen says it's my husband.
If I answer, I'll cry. Voicemail takes it.
"God no," says Brianna. "We hate each other,
right, Just? Never date the competition,
you destroy your luck. Besides." She starts
morosely high-fiving again. "I'm a virgin."
Justin laughs. She wraps her hair around her face
to smell it. "I pay attention in class.
Professor Krugman, he's a real professor."
She points at a headline I just kicked. **Housing**
Upturn Predicted. "He says housing increases

don't matter in the long run. It's a blip,
if it's even a blip. If I don't get a job,
it's Wharton MBA. Or teach English in Japan.
But this girl on my floor told me Asian girls
depilate their whole bodies, even their arms.
I can't be the hairiest person in my life."

What will I do next year without the job
I don't want? I sleep. "Hey!" says Brianna.
"I could go back to Spain, smoke Ducados
in *okupa* cafes. Be a poet!
Sorry." Laughs herself out of last tears
at the idea. "I didn't mean to get all
Sylvia Plathy on you. Anyway, my trust fund
is safe. Knock plastic." She reaches to rap the tie
Justin hung over the seat. I say, "In Madrid
workers smoke Ducados. Reds are for Anarchista
Eurotrash wannabes." Brianna lips the cigarette
she'll light on the platform. "I'll have my portfolio
next week, promise." All semester she's revised
following precisely, appallingly, my suggestions.
She says "Think of me as raw talent wasted."
I'm pissed I think of her at all. Justin again,
talking at no one: "Merrill Lynch says
what interests you in our company. I'm amped.
I'm whipped. I'm like 'Um, I heard you were hiring?'
Nah, I'm giving him eight good reasons.
He cuts me off. . . ." The train slows, surceases
with a hiss. Fifteen responsible children
stand in the aisle. *Jizz, jess, fuck,* markered
on seats by younger, irresponsible children.

Off the train, Justin jumps into a low Mazda coupe,
yellow as Dick Tracy's hat, parked unticketed

at an expired meter, open to the rain. I autodial:
"I'm at the station. Don't come, I need the walk."
Brianna: "Where's Soon-Ji anyway? Flying his plane back?
God, what'll we do if nobody wants us?"
Justin: "Soon-Ji will fucking keep us I guess.
All we have is Dad's money."
Brianna: "Mine's Mom's. Half of it gone in the crash.
But Soon-Ji is great-grandfathered in. He'll be richer
than we'll ever be if he never gets a job at all."
Justin: "Professor, you hand back comments tomorrow,
right? They're important to me."
"Fuck you, suck-up," Brianna says.

Sometimes I forget I'm pregnant till I walk.
Brianna vaults into the car, leans out:
"Want a ride, Professor? Cigarette?"
She puts one in my mouth, lights it
with a naked boy lighter that squirts fire
out his tiny penis. "Beer?" Tears a can
off a six-pack choke-ring, sticks it in a baggie
she pulls from Justin's glove compartment,
pops the top, shoves it in my hand. "Now
you can't walk home—pregnant, smoking,
carrying a beer? You'd be arrested. Anyway,
Soon-Ji is having a party. Cristal! Rappers!
He produces them and brings his stable
down from Queens. You have to come!
He was going to take your workshop,
he admires you, but took playwriting instead."
For final relaxation in prenatal yoga, we do
our kegels squatting in a circle, shut-eyed—
"for perineal strengthening," the teacher said.
Then we lie on our sides, breathe in, breathe out,
bellies like dropped anchors on the floor.

Our muscles tick, smoothing, loosening.
The teacher reads an affirming poem. I tense up.

Brianna: "We always say Krugman's one of the few
Professors we'd friend on Facebook.
But, Daisy, we'd friend you too." Memory:
Favorite Teachers at our college house parties,
slow-dancing with us, doing lines
in our bathrooms. When are they going to grow up,
we said. I wave, walk, drop the cigarette
in the beer, the can in the trashcan, relieved
to be embarrassed, triumphant, sorry. Justin
drives along beside me, Brianna rides shotgun
standing like a surfer on a breaking wave.
Justin—"Fuck"—floors it, roars past me, away.
I don't know how to end this poem. On "Torment"
I wrote: "You may want to find a way to suggest
ironic distance between the poet and speaker."
I couldn't figure out what else,
to responsible children, there was to say.

II

Women's Poetry

I, too, dislike it.
However,

                    I was trying to not think
when out of the gaping wound
of the car-detailing garage (smells like metallic sex)
came a Nissan GT-R fitted with an oversized spoiler.
Backing out sounded like clearing the throat of god.
A gold snake zizzed around the license plate.
Sunburst hubcaps, fancy undercarriage installation
casting a pool of violet light on the pocked pavement
of gum blots. Was it this that filled me with desire?

Midnight Feeding

The open shed on the lawn's far side stinks of gas
from the hateful mower that pulls me where it wants
when I mow, which is seldom. I rip up grass.
Humid night's moon's nothing-halo; the lawn pretends
to candy floss. Black-white dud roses dead since June,
alive enough to scratch my bare legs. I'm wearing nothing
but underpants, flipflops. Arms full, I stumble out,
flashlight in my mouth, turn my head to choose
what's lit. Inside the dirt-floor shed, I fill bowls:
Dry bits, tuna slop. The flashlight hurts my mouth
till I drop it, dwindles into its cone where it falls to blight
a denticular leaf.
              "Raphael! Gabriel! Lucifer!" Feral
kittens come running, vicious, filthy. Hum of the road.
Uriel shines his reflector-eyes from among mower parts
in the shed's darkest corner. Disgust shakes his paw.
He won't get close since wild La Mamma ran off weeks ago.
My three-month daughter cries on the baby monitor
I wear like a Miss America sash. She'll wait,
Uriel must eat. Can't leave them. Coons or coyotes
would get the food and kittens too. My fur rises
on my arms. What a bad mom! Also, I refuse
to look at the stars. There are too many
stars in poems you have to get drunk to write.

Kissinger at the Louvre (Three Drafts)

1

Kissinger in black-tie shuffles to the town car
idling at the museum complex edge
between where the glum Pei pyramid rises
and the gardens begin. "Is that—" I say,
and "Yes," says Jim, baby in his arms,
me shoving the empty stroller to get home
by naptime. Nobody notices, clicking
at each other through camera phones, Kissinger
looking matchlessly neat, clean, ugly and
dressed by servants. His driver's at the door,
arms stretched wide as in a fish-this-big tall tale
in welcome. The ear-wired bodyguard,
hand on Kissinger's gray-fur head so it won't
scrape the door-frame, bends him into the car.

If I were a different kind of poet, I'd put
Kissinger in front of *The Raft of the Medusa*
blinking at the father weeping for his son
lying dead over his lap as the sails
of the ship that will rescue them are
sighted on the horizon and the top man
in the spout of survivors waves his ragged
undershirt. Or I'd put him gazing reflectively
at *The Death of Sardanapalus*, a Potentate
presiding amid an exorbitance of fabrics
over his imminent suicide by fire,
slaves bringing in, in order of importance,
horses, gems, plate and favored concubines
for slaughter. I'm not that kind of poet.

2

Kissinger totters befuddled by culpability,
luncheon champagne and dotage. The car

eats him. I won't pretend the bodyguard's
Vietnamese or Cambodian, though that's
the obvious truth-in-lies move—he's French,
that ratface-handsome, smoked-out look—
and doesn't care *merde* for history. He makes
the old man bow, same move with which
the beat cop, our public servant, submits
the petty criminal to the patrol car,
same move the anguished teenager got—
half-protective, half-corrective or coercive,
half-kind—after the arraignment for leaving
her newborn to die in a rest stop dumpster.

Anybody can understand the girl, and even
the purse-snatcher. Bodyguard bends Kissinger
gently in, portly little Kissinger, gloves his head—
anything hurt will be the hand of the servant.
Ecru upholstery with oxblood accents, minibar
something like a safe, CNN muted to newscrawl
and the anchor's frozen-flesh face. The latest assistant,
gender irrelevant, busy with a BlackBerry across from him,
root beer-colored eyes and preternaturally neat hair
of *La belle ferronière*, keeps the lap desk, emergency
Magic Wand Stain Remover Stick, eyebrow brush
and dossier of Opinions in what looks like
"the football"—the nuclear war plan suitcase
Presidential aides carry at all times—but isn't.

   3

The one camera flash as he got in
gave Kissinger a headache. As they start
for his Avenue du President Wilson hotel,
the Rue de Rivoli sliding by in a haze,
he falls uncomfortably asleep to the anodyne

glow and murmur (*"tournez à gauche"*) of the driver's
GPS device. The relieved assistant
opens an Imagist anthology. In Osaka, Oslo or Wasilla,
Alaska some weeks later, a woman at her kitchen table
uploads Paris vacation photos to her laptop.
"Who's that behind me?" A dark figure. "He looks familiar."
"How should I know," says her husband.
"I'm trying to get Baby to eat more potato."
"Oh well. I look fat in it," she says. And deletes.

Thrash

      Twenty years ago, I squeezed
onto the edge of the Knights of Columbus
stage to escape a lot of leaping, bashing bodies
as Hüsker Du did "Eight Miles High"
and Jeff shielded May with his tallish
body and she slam-danced inside the frame
of him. That's all. Afterwards on the liquid
city street the screeching still running
up and down my veins, I was going to help
May when she was going to smash her head
into the belly of a frat boy who laughed
at us except after all he didn't
want to get into it and walked away.
The world's repeatedly saved by people
whether right or wrong just goddammit
not wanting to get into it.

Econo Motel, Ocean City

Korean monster movie on the SyFy channel,
lurid Dora the Explorer blanket draped tentlike
over Baby's portacrib to shield us from unearned
innocence. The monster slings its carapace
in reverse swan dive up the embankment, triple-jointed bug legs
clattering, bathroom door ajar, exhaust roaring,
both of us naked, monster chomps
fast food stands, all that quilted aluminum, eats through streams
of running people, the promiscuously cheerful guilty American
scientist dies horribly. Grease-dusted ceiling fan
paddles erratically, two spars missing. Sheets whirled
to the polluted rug. I reach under the bed, fish out
somebody else's crunched beer can, my forearm comes out
dirty. Monster brachiates from bridge girders like a gibbon
looping round and around uneven bars, those are your fingers
in my tangles or my fingers, my head hangs
half off the king-size, monster takes tiny child actor
to its bone stash. Pillow's wet. The warped ceiling mirror
makes us look like fat porno dwarfs
in centripetal silver nitrate ripples. My glasses on the side table
tipped onto scratchproof lenses, earpieces sticking up
like arms out of disaster rubble. Your feet hooked over my feet. What
    miasma
lays gold dander down on forms of temporary
survivors wandering the promenade? You pull Dora
back over us—Baby's dead to the world—intrude
your propagandistic intimacy jokes,
unforgiving. "What, in a motel room?" I say.
Purple clouds roll back to reveal Armageddon
a dream in bad digital unreality. Explosions repeat patterns like
fake flames dance on fake fireplace logs. Sad Armageddon
of marriage: how pretty much nice
we meant to be, and couldn't make a difference.

Ippopotamo

assisted readymade, La Specola, Florence

You are looking to a specimen
whose exact age is unknown,
but it must be ca. 300 years old
as it probably lived in the Boboli Gardens
during the reign of Cosimo III de' Medici
(1670–1723).

It is still visible the mark of the rope,
the sign of its captivity,
around its neck.

The hippopotamus is reported
in the Giovanni Targioni Tozzetti's catalogue,
compiled in 1763, and it is almost certainly
one of the oldest specimens
displayed in the Museum.

Its age is also revealed
by the clumsy execution
of the stuffing and mounting,
and through the animal's expression.

It was likely not observed alive
as the legs are mounted as a plantigrade
    walks with entire sole of the foot
    touching the ground
although it is a digitigrade
    walks so that only toes
    touch the ground

    Detritus of empire,
    mouth awkwardly gaped,
    threatening, the corners
    beginning to tear, too many teeth shoved in.

A Snow Woman

A window on a side yard in winter.
I'm reading Stevens, as usual not into it.
I decide again not to get pregnant.
The neighbor child's sandbox still out there,
lid on underneath snow: White barrow
burial for troubled life's
embraces. Romance: I see them:
Upstairs-Jeff begins a snowman
with Thérèse and the kid, and we go out and help and
we're in an Eddie Bauer winter catalogue,
dumping snow on one another to show
we're harmless, grinning with open mouths.
Parsnip nose, jalapeño smile, habañero eyes.
Thérèse's sloppy velvet hat. "Regardes, Doudou,"
Thérèse just-tenured in the French department
(specialty Valéry), "la bonfemme de neige!"
Doudou flails, struggles, nearly two, down out
of Maman's arms, drives a fist deep into
the snow woman's middle, right deep
into it. One must have a womb of snow,
an eye of cold. One must have a blue bright beret.
Un long regard sur le calme des dieux!

This Need Not Be a Comment on Death

There's my three-year-old mom c. 1942
in the flickery movie digitized to video:
Slippery blond hair, you can tell from the
light of it though the film's black and
white, squiggling the little chunk of her in
her tank suit, sand drizzling from her
knees, her own handsome mom, dead
of cancer 1949, co-author of "Direct
Observation as a Research Method" and
"Children and War," smiling on a dock.
This need not be a comment on death

because after all my mother puts her
fingers through my hair when I'm in
labor. Contractions are jagged spikes on
the monitor screen: The nurse turned the
Pitocin up. My daughter's heart zigzags its
own hectic graph, a cartoon mountain
range scribbled in quick. "Your hair's
always full of knots," my mother says.
Never a caress without a complaint. Dry
air of grimly clean birth suite saps my
mind, skin. *Needs more joy*, I think, quite
cold, but don't feel pain when "fuck my
hair," I say, and my mother, a plotline,
leaves to wait at the B&B for news of her
granddaughter. If she never said it? If I
imagined it? If she was being kind? *You'll
want to remember every minute of your birth
story, and every birth story's a great one,* the
midwife said. After thirty hours labor even
the epidural can't keep me awake, even
hanging on the squat bar with the extent of
my upper body strength. A plotline,
I stop trying to push my daughter fully,
completely, desperately out, and she's born.

Here's the refrigerator I dragged from the wall
to see what's buzzing: A tiny toy robot bug
crawled back there when my rarely crying
daughter set it, legs churning, on the floor.
And here am I, plotline who gave birth to her,
hauling fridge desperately backward by edges.
"Happy tears!" she shouts, angrily smearing
with slashing curve of arm the bumpy mound
of her face. "I'm stoic!" A word I taught her
by accident when "she's stoic," I told my husband
the first time she fell from the high slide

and refused to cry. "Stoic" crawled its legs
and body into the refrigerator of her brain
and stuck. My arms as far around the fridge
as they'll go: I pull, pant, I groan, leave squalid
grease tracks on our gouged linoleum.
The plug extracts itself from the socket,
rebounds clanging the coil; the bug driving
its blind head forward won't squiggle free.
"It has to run down and get quiet that way."
I crouch to wipe my stoic's face with
my sweat-wet sweatshirt, her fingers in my
hair, she bites at it, flops back on linoleum.
"It's talking and dead," she says, fascinated.
Me exasperated. "I'll buy you a new one."
Here's the debacle. I can't push the fridge
back. It sits, an abandoned barracks
in the pale field of the kitchen. A sigh, trickle,
a cracking sound. "Why does everything die?"
Her anger. "Why do *I* have to die." A spike of
outrage as faint buzzing not all that furious
under the refrigerator fails to finish, as,
like a glacier calving, freezer ice falls free.

The poem's narrow shape actually resembles an icebox . . .
Camille Paglia on William Carlos Williams' "This Is Just to Say"

Lyric

A woman crying on the phone in her Marketplace flower kiosk,
turning her velvety back on a customer trying to give her money
among the daffodil purple pink hyacinth yellow pansy mob; and

a drunk girl Irish step dancing for St. Patrick's Day festooned
with cardboard glitter shamrocks at the corner of Main Street and Asylum;
her form's first rate; eyes and dishevelment say she's toasted; and

my daughter sits legs straight out on the floor deep into her dialogue
for Bad Pig and Good Princess: "'*Hocus pocus, be dead,' he said,
but she jumped up and said 'I SAID, don't bother me with that dying!'*"

Gas price up again, stink of gouging. In Hartford, Cabela's—World's
Foremost Outdoor Outfitter—is a modernist gun megachurch
between interstate off-ramps. A bronze deer freezes mid-leap out front, and

rainy twilit parking lines give off geometric glow. Inside, a fake mountain
rising far up to the ceiling. Stuffed wolves, lynx, stoat, white-tailed deer,
    ocelot
sniffingly posed among cardboard crags. Shopping carts and shoppers

double-wide in double-wide aisles, and strong: A heavyweight Amazon
pulls back the string of a hunting bow like pulling clingwrap
from the tube. Her camouflage is Deciduous Winter Forest Mix. Everything

wood-grained plastic except oxblood walnut gunstocks ensconced on racks
on racks on racks. Goose calls in a box, turkey decoys in duck blinds; and
butcher tools: $69.95 the 14 piece lot: gloves, shears, swing blade, bone

saw, gutter, cutting board in attractive monogrammable sheath
like a laptop case. And reality punches its way out of the lyric: My phone
rings, news from my sister: "*We're getting divorced. I want full custody.*"

Automatically in my mind I side against her, murmur um-hmms, oh-no's,
tsk-tsks, lose myself in non-reflections of concrete things. Woman buys
    bandsaw
for her basement: *"No more paying the butcher an arm and a leg!"* A display

of tents through which my daughter reappears, disappears, arms flailing joy.
"I told him 'I don't know if I could love you after this.'" My sister in my ear.
Escalator inexorable beside the mountain whirs its upward always upward
    song.

Stolen Vehicle Discovered at the Junkyard

a wheel, an axle gone, wires sticking out
of the hacked-open steering column like stamens
of exotic flowers.   Don't want it back.   I see now
all I've ever wanted in life is to push the button on the EZ crusher,
watch the weight come down and my old van windows
like spurts of green water like glass.

Inside All This

Worn Eeyore in lavender, fur on Tigger
abrading. The tag sale mobile dangles
its dolls and mirrors.
                        Inside all this,
a baby laid on its stomach, irritably
scraping its face back and forth in its sleep,
snail trails of snot widening and widening
on its eczema'd face and over the sheets
like soap the squeegee man fans
on the outside of a store window till
the baby's nearly awake in fear or rage
or half-consciousness (which are only all need)
so you pick it up before it wakes
in time to fold it in the darkness of your body—
it cries awake anyway, because you were so happy
you picked it up before it cried, because wrestling
up out of sleep comes from nowhere in the mind
like the whooped-up druggy partying of soldiers
behind a sieged barricade, because otherwise dying,
or something, gets remembered.

> *bring me to the singing place*
> *bring me to the singing place*
> *bring me to the singing place*
> *locks on doors, bolts shoot loose*
> *big bare hands on bare big shoulders*

Il Penseroso: The Fat Lady

"Can't talk," I say, doing 85. "Can't hear
or talk." I snap shut the phone,
cut him off, hold the dead phone
to my ear like a hankie-wrapped
ice-pack to a contusion. I slow to 70;
the fat lady I cut off at the onramp
shouts through both our closed windows
so wide her mouth's all teeth and
tongue and dark and her Jesus-fish
and troop loop ride away, I-95 rushing
up too superreal like a movie-promo
before digital got finesse. Green highway
signs only tell how to get where you
already know to go. Used car lots
flash by like jewelers' windows;
last pale sheets of sun dribble away
as evening finds its shape against
the things of the ground,
loses shape becoming night—

She was tired of sad modern endings.
She was tired of modern sadness and ennui.
She narrated things calmly and swiftly
like an easy-running stream
beneath the racing jumping flux—
unnatural this hum of narration,
the way the sun's unnatural—unreal—
she wanted 19th-century endings—
believably happy wives—
turn the radio louder . . .
the problem might be she calls herself "she" . . .

so they bleed, I'm toothing
dry skin off my lips, dropping the phone

on the car floor under the brake—
oil refineries are nets and
scaffolding set far back
from the road—and everywhere,
tire-tread shorn from truck-wheels,
collars and cuffs ripped free
and never swept up, washed up
along and leaning against and kissing
at the median strip, jumps up
to twang the chassis—I duck down,
pick up the phone, the car sways,
I hit redial, can't stop choking—
"Look," I say. "I won't say sorry.
It's nothing either of us did. Can't we
just move on from here?"—"Can't talk,"
he says, hangs up. No static. Smooth
techno-silence like a moral that's
big, bigger than the road is fast.

How his hair lifts and falls. Ahead,
an explosion: *brake-lights*
sequentially burn back at her,
smoke pouf becomes a skein
they all drive through: an
18-wheeler's tire has blown
apart and now the truck limps
shedding tread that minivans,
Hyundais, Escapes, H2s swerve
to avoid, graceful conga
line of cars.
            She saw this driving
along, the veins of her breasts
the same blue as old roads, the cars
drag their red lights, movable

puddles, behind them. The injured
truck clunks along the shoulder
toward the rest-stop ramp, tire
clinging to the back wheel rim
coming loose, whapping, slapping,
whacking the ground, like a wife
pounding her pillow, alone all night.

Elegy

in memory D. K., Scrovegni Chapel, Padua

"Even Duccio can't match
Giotto's stage management of great tragedy":
Transgendered Professor Y in leather miniskirt
paces before the screen, wood pointer
scraping saint faces, slapping
hunched women of the Lamentation.
Blue-gold tumult of the chapel walls.
After-lunch lecture hall heat.
You're in that class with me. We go on
from there—not long. You do "The Waste Land"
in different voices—*Come in under the shadow*
of that red rock—Strom Thurmond, Aussie
bartender, Cantonese. *HURRY UP PLEASE*
ITS TIME. Twenty years later,
I get your news by Facebook update,
three hundred characters or less,
waiting for the Scrovegni to open
in the windy square across from
Donatello's horse-and-rider,
dust flecks foaming past fetlocks
and stirrups. You're someone I slept with
long ago, stopped, pitied, forgot.
Some remember the Berlin Wall,
some remember Vietnam or the first Gulf War,
I don't remember you except standing
by my chair in the smelly bedroom,
blue sheets undone. You scrub at your head
wet from the shower, drop the towel
on the floor. You ice my earlobe, light a match
to sterilize the needle: *Give me a small red new potato,*
you say. *Kev pierced my ear with a needle and potato.*
We were drunk, maybe tripping. Mom was waiting

when I came in, 3 a.m., and saw the blood. . . . You jab.
No pain. A tearing through resistance,
tissues numbly separating. You do your mom:
JesusMaryandJoseph! she screamed. Have mercy!

Liberalism

Sneaker-squeak on gym floor, referee whistle—
sounds of sound stopping. Everybody hears
and knows this: Indoor light, mildew smell
of old towel. Empty gym and the team practicing.
Like a tabletop aquarium tank with a few sick
hardy fish surviving; the deep-sea diver,
feet planted in acid-color poprock pebbles,
blows bubbles bluely upward. The power forward's
boyfriend highlights page after textbook page
(American History from World War II: Vietnam
through the Reagan era this week—Mrs. Dugan's
a Jimmy Carter fan so she'll linger a whole day there)
under reinforced windows on a high bleacher
unknowing, bored, resisting inside the system.

Perpetual Youth Lost by Humankind

Fontainebleau

Chateau

"Boar season," says the woman who serves us
coffee, exhausting her English. Not
what was promised. Not enough paintings
in the chateau. Only Rosso Fiorentino
frescoes, inscrutable stories' inscrutable morals, *Perpetual
Youth Lost by Humankind* wasted by restoration:
An ash-hued naked lady slumps ass-back
by a river (something Acheron about it)
to kiss a beast half-lion half-swan, which is
sometimes how I think of you. One king ordered them
painted over, another scraped them up again
from layers they got lost under. "Don't like these Rossos"—
"Like's not the point." So effaced, refined, refixed—
"Don't fucking hold my hand if you fucking don't like me"—
now nothing meant means nothing new.

Garden

Not what you said. Garden of Diana
half in the chateau shadow. The sun in January
hot. Truce. Wild grapes hang beady among
gray leaves. Give me your hope
and your hand, your hair flying fast
in my face, think of walking
on gravel how nice with the river
running west. Too maudlin,
a fact, I'm too young, I know
how the hairs on your legs and chest
curl and I like it. Locals on benches eat
baguettes stuffed with Brie. In the fountain,
four dogs piss four directions; on her pedestal above, Diana, blasé
oh, hmm, dogs do piss. Boneless hand fiddles
in her stag's many-pointed antlers. Four

bronze penises spit and burble; wind turns the streams.
Sourness a kind of joy I try for intricately.
I flex my feet, try to draw the dogs—can't do piss or penises.
"Remote from real experience."

Forest

A walk in the forest, how to be all of us. This is
not the kind of light that slaps you but filters
dust low between winter trees softly. Getting on towards sundown.
Sour grape taste on my tongue, alive, awake,
something so wild so meager, and yet . . .
Chasse en cours, signs say, nailed
to trees and hung on sawhorses. *Merci pour
votre comprehension.* When across
the forest path far ahead where the terrain
lifts to the gorge—remote suddenness—
a herd of wild boar stampedes out of the brush
back into the brush—too many to count. One behind
the other, boar-script across the page of the forest,
snout to haunch. Your face appears to me
all red on one side. We won't remember
changing. Black as paper dolls held up against
a washing light, boar pitch like boats on an ocean. We kept
on breathing. Nothing left of the smell when we
reached the running-place. The idea of their intentness
in running, like children working over a crayon drawing,
scribbling till they ruin it with revision.
We heard nothing. Empty
light and silence! Not what we came for.

Metaphor for Something, or
Solving the Credit Crunch

                                    Door slam wakeup:
                                A half-sighing unmoist
                                Philadelphia sinus sniff
                                announces a guy in a red,
                                white and blue seersucker
                                suit who parks on our block
                                every 6 a.m. to walk to work.
                                He likes a dumb bumper joke
                                —his magnet loop which says
                                Support Lap Dancing. New today
                                is a gag half hockey puck glued
                                to his Ford 150 rear window
                                amid a decal of spiderwork
                                cracks radiating across the
                                shadowy defroster strips
                                as if the puck's halfway
                                through the glass—
                                but isn't.

His Failed Band, 1973

Stands in a silly jacket at a lakeshore,
half-dense pine woods, narrow-chested Bob
in horizontal stripes, the only one with his head
above a horizon of slight hills across water
misty as a memory of bad feelings evaporating.
Lou sly in moustache keeping it in. Shaggy Ellis
looks at water not the camera. Rick facing front
in light-colored sneaks coming out from the rock-
littered shoreline path, hands not quite fists
at his side, sloppy happy grin says he's had a few,
hasn't gotten any. Four buddies arranged
on a diagonal like on an album cover
that never got made. Overcast dawn half-light.
Hair not so kempt as usually found in photos
however candid these days. Disturbing no one.

The Spirit Award

Most Valuable, Most Improved, and for least valuable unimprovables,
the Spirit Award. Skinny in my T-back,
I got Most Valuables. Swimming mostly hurt. My shoulders
are still big from this.
                              The chrome-look figures on the trophies
were crudely modeled. Some trained artist
hunched at her rotating pedestal in her high-ceilinged studio,
flicked at the clay with small picks, wire loops. She shrugged and rolled her
     shoulders,
trying to get it right—but it's wrong, the pose, legs fused
into one leg, only a cheated indentation between, like symbols
on public bathrooms telling Ladies or Gents.
                                        The trophy diver
leans slightly forward at the waist, scrawny arms winged out,
gazes moony at the far deep, closed lips curved into a Mona Lisa.
Not much shoulder, narrow torso, sloping mass of breasts
bigger than you'd see on most swimmers with their breasts like muscley
     knots.
I quit at puberty: Never managed to swim hard enough to swim mine away.

No one dives like that at a swim meet. You stand doubled over
on the block in the echoing room, hands gripping the lip by your feet till
     your hands hurt,
you feet shoulder's width apart, loose and tense—loose with adrenaline
waiting for the instant the pistol fires; tensely ready, a spring
wound tight, you explode outward
body a circumflex above the sentence of the pool. Enter shallow . . .
glide into your stroke, water like mercury—
it divides, springs away.
                              Maybe they dove like the trophies sixty years ago,
                    baggy-suited
and, for the times, immodest. The war over, economy rising,
House UnAmericans beginning—which is also an ending. Movies
spring into color! Esther Williams backstrokes in lipstick,

look up the clips on YouTube. She slides heavy-hipped
through flower-strewn pools, hardly raises a splash. Frank O'Hara
is home from the South Seas: At Harvard, V.A.-funded,
his poems ahead of him not yet talking
to the sun at Key West, his liver
not yet enlarged. Simone De Beauvoir traveling
America, falling in love with Nelson Algren,
describing the U.S. in pronouncements
mostly pissed and mostly true.

Her Failed Band, 1982

Black lace mantilla yes but she calls it her Guyville
Headbanger Act. She's leaning quasi-
        raunchy elbows on the end of a plywood crate. Her crazy-shaped
        guitar sparkles turquoise, well, look at the date, always a riff
    on or homage to the sixties. It's Reagan,
Tylenol poisoning, Falklands, lipo, Ma Bell split.
It's everything, and everything stays there.

L'Allegro: Driving Home

Must I change my triumphant songs? said I to myself,
Must I indeed learn to chant the cold dirges of the baffled,
And sullen hymns of defeat?

—Walt Whitman, "Year That Trembled and Reel'd Beneath Me"

Considering flesh, my body pushing back the carseat,
speeding behind storm steaming and tailing away
faster than I can drive. Setting sun behind me
cracks open over southwest suburbs, November
spilling light to flash sides of glassy Philly skyline:
Molten silver holding building shapes, also greeny.
I made one boy almost cry today.
Made one almost cry!
Billboard for the Pilots Union: *Severe Turbulence Ahead:*
Lightning wraps a plane like a spiderweb a fly:
Five years without a contract. Fly into that would you?
Thinking about you. Twilight indigo
and intensifying. Considering public artwork
(1% of all building projects by law),
a sideways spotlit space capsule
by a cut-rate depression-era retro-futurist
on top of the highwayside bank building
that changed its name in the last most hostile takeover.
Brushing aside the poison pill.
A boy who said: "Tell me how I can ace this course."
Public art stinks always but a certain participation
in the style of the day before yesterday cannot be denied.
Windy: Big trucks swinging their trailers
almost into my lane. I blow with them. Said I to myself,
Have you given thought that what you want is options
and considered nakedness and putting your heart away?
Have you felt hurt? Given advice?
What were you thinking, throwing things headward?
Telling a boy: "Write." Wishing I could.
Nothing but months, weeks of jots, miscarriages.
Gusts coming in over Tinicum Nature

Preserve, Enterprise and Island Avenues.
Airport: Amber lights in the eastern sky:
Jets spaced equidistant and reeling in
as if hooked along an invisible fishline.
The Walt Whitman Bridge's shivery misty girders.
Thinking: What's it matter?
Saying: "This won't affect your final grade."
Nothing affects. Looking forward to
you with your cronies and ethics violations
I brush my teeth in the car. Nowhere to spit.
Gusts across bare spaces between stadiums.

Attenti Agli Zingari[*]

Pretty baby, you look so heavenly . . .
—Blondie

1. *Odori, Ospitalità*

What happened to Blanca? What happened to Rome?
Is it happening to me?
                    2004, Blanca the Gypsy
looks six,
rubbing against men, rubbing against women
at the no-name Caffé with red plastic chairs.
Her name can't be Blanca, everybody calls her Blanca.
She cadges money and cigarettes, kisses my hair,
steals my colored pencils. Little bird nose,
pretty smile, pain in the ass. I'm thinking about
getting pregnant.
                    2007, Blanca sleazy, writhing,
adorable, ignores me, chats with men
who pat her face and belly. At the produce stand,
the Nigerian fruit seller yearns at a Ferrari
idling curbside. Blanca shivers and snickers
when he puppy-scratches behind her ears,
play-slaps her cheek. The Ferrari backs
down the Piazzale, farting into Rome traffic.
The color is *argento titano* (titanium silver);
costs—I looked it up—€185,000 base. I love
that its noise says *who has the money deserves me.*
Blanca palms an enormous comice.
The fruit seller bellows, she bites to ruin it,
he stamps at her, she weighs it in her hand,
walks smirking away. He mutters
back to his cashbox, sucking his lip
up under his nose, chops *odori* for *minestra.*
                                Yesterday
the wife of a naval officer was robbed,

---

[*] Graffiti on a tree in Rome: *Beware of the Gypsies.*

raped and murdered in this neighborhood.
A Gypsy is arrested. *Animali!* says the mayor.
Nessuna ospitalità a questi animali! say crude posters
in ugly red writing, flaunting the Fascist tricolor flame.
Gypsies are beaten in the street. The government
of ex-Communist Romano Prodi loads Gypsies in buses,
returns them to Romania. Overnight, all Rome's
beggars are gone. We'll never see Blanca again.
This is not a tragedy, it only feels somehow pointlessly sad.
Empty Gypsy camps are bulldozed by the authorities.
A stench of casual outdoor shitting remains.
The dollar hits 1.40 against the Euro. I turn 40.
Maisie's eleven months old.

2. Padlocks, Suicidal

Padlocks multiply on the footbridge Ponte Milvio.
They look like a swarm of bees that shine,
clipped to chains, clipped to one another.
A novel began it: Lovers wrote their initials
on a lock, attached it to a lamppost,
threw the key in the Tiber. Lovesick or loving,
copycats followed. *We must keep this new tradition alive,*
said the mayor when lock-weight pulled
a lamppost down. A Mafia construction company
donated stronger poles and cement.
Padlocks of love puddle on the ground.
Bangladeshis—Rome tolerates its illegals—
arrange locks for sale on crates. A girl buys
the smallest, €1, thumbnail size, surrounded
by her girl gang, no lover necessary,
giggling like the barely burbling river,
then solemn, smoothing back curl-edged hair.
Rita! scream her friends when her key twinkles, falling.
A goth couple grinds and kisses, flesh-fat showing
through intentional rips in grommet-spangled jeans,
grackle-colored hair mingling. Two men in suits
tongue each other's teeth. The Nigerian's radio sings
beautiful girls, they'll have you suicidal.

3. *Sunday Morning, Night*

Smashed beer bottles, crunched Marlboro packs
with *FUMO UCCIDE* in enormous letters
across the front. *Rita-Gianni sempre*
in permanent marker, glitter pink nailpolish hearts
underneath. Love-lock graffiti
has wiped out all others. No more *USA merda,*
circled *A*, hammer and sickle, Fascist rifle sight,
not even (*Napoli merda*) soccerfan jeers.
Workers in maroon and orange jumpsuits
painstakingly scrub the bridge clean. *Rita-Gianni*
is back before they're halfway across.

Slow Italian day waning, apartment blocks cut up
silver dusk, sparrows fly rearing and bucking
past construction cranes, shimmering Tinkertoys
laboring into evening. The yellow crane
unspools wire cord, bows to lower
a parcel of I-beams. The sparrows fly
over the junkyard, the New York Steakhouse,
they funnel and swoop past the sports bar,
Smart Car dealer, truck bed full of flowers
and porcini, past the girl on the parked motorcycle
sitting sidesaddle the better to show
the clean yellow triangle of underpants.
Swirl down among Tiber plane trees'
blurry camouflage. Maisie zoning
in her cut-rate stroller that sticks on bridge stones
laid down fan-form. "Birdie!" She jerks alert,
points. Knees locked, body arched. Birds shriek
panicked apart, contract en masse
into an umbrella pine's black-green deepnesses,
crazed every time the sun goes down,
thinking it won't rise again.

4. Histories: Umbrellas

Rare days of rain, lock-vendors
sell €5 umbrellas by the bridge, water streaming
down their faces. 312 A.D., Constantine
saw a dream-cross in the sky, defeated Maxentius
at Ponte Milvio, threw him in the Tiber
where he drowned. In 1849 Garibaldi blew up Milvio
to keep the French out of Rome, lost
the revolution anyway. Umbrellas smoke
in the downpour. Kenneth Rexroth, c. 1949
rode in on his bike: "The Tiber appears, and then a sign /
'PONTE MILVIO.' We enter / Rome in the tracks of the first /
Triumph of barbarism and religion." My umbrella blows to pieces,
most times, halfway across the bridge.
I buy another on the other side.

5. *Shame and Go Home, 2004*

A year into Iraq Bush arrives in Rome.
The huge cheerful protest march winds
past Campidoglio, Colosseo, il Foro,
Circo Massimo and the Baths of Caracalla,
a better tour of ancient Rome than any bus.
We walk with a Norwegian couple, naming ourselves
Tourists Against the War. The Norwegians are surprised
we speak "pretty grammatical English for Americans"
and know as much as they do about U.S. politics
politely ignoring that we can't—and they can—
recite the names of every member of Bush's cabinet.
Bush as monkey, Bush as Hitler, Berlusconi as Mussolini.
American flags with swastikas painted on,
signs of the times.
Buttar giu il governo del neoduce!
Buttiamoli giu! Bush vergonati e vai a casa!
Throw the bums out. Shame and go home.
Pictures from Abu-Ghraib photoshopped to show Bush grinning
over a pile of naked bodies, Condoleeza Rice holding a prisoner on a
    leash.
Cheney urging a dog to attack a man's naked crotch.

Attenti agli Zingari::   Woman in prolific skirt, hitched hook-and-eye
at her hips, little mirrors sewn in. Doped
mosquito-bit baby, sleepily sucking in her lap,
foot of the down escalators, Flaminio Metro station.

Man in the doorway of a church,
collecting rice thrown after weddings,
sieving it for cigarette butts.

Beggar woman kneeling unmoving in July sun,
ass in the air, face to pavement,
weirdly clean fingernails,
neatly manicured little crescent moons,
peeks sideways to see who's coming.

Prepubescent boy plays accordion
on the tram, small and sulky in a wifebeater,
"Never on Sunday" virtuoso.
He raises his arms.
Armpits of thick black man-hair.

6. Histories: 2000. July

My first time in Rome, our honeymoon, a cheerful place,
Jubilee year: Slaves and prisoners are released,
debts forgiven, God's mercies particularly manifest
and Catholics are absolved of their sins
if they walk to all seven basilicas. They troop
in footsore double group-tour lines behind a woman
holding aloft a pink umbrella. She murmurs facts
to her mic; they wear headset receivers.
There's no more cacophony in art places,
just watery hiss of tourguide whisper.
In the Palazzo Doria Pamphili,
Mary, resting on the flight to Egypt,
bends wearily over her foursquare baby,
his tiny penis pointing from the canvas
innocent and clean as a cap gun.
"Are you hungry, Sister?" says a fat guy to a nun.
"Would you like some McDonalds?" History
hasn't happened yet. On the crowded flight home
I sit next to a Texan who's never been out of Texas before,
she went to Lourdes, then Rome. She's sinless.
We fly over New York, *selva oscura*:
"What are those two tall buildings down there?"

7. *Song, 2007. Camp X-Ray Cages*

Men in orange jumpsuits.
Fingers laced through the fencing.
Via Flaminia Vecchia graffiti: *Dux mea lux.*
Hope it doesn't mean Duce, my light.
I get scared, writes someone
in the London Review of Books,
when I see Fascists demonstrate,
though I know they're only a small percentage
of the population.
The sky seems a kind of wallpaper.
The river a moving screen.
The bird-strung bridges are where we feel the air.
Trivia question: Where is Blanca now?

8. *Argento Titano. Now Dusk Purple*

Can't cross the bridge. Dusk. Forza Nuova,
the refounded Fascists, demonstrate at the other end.
No agli zingari! they chant, joyous,
in their phalanx or tight scrum. *Zingari* might
or might not be as bad as yelling
nigger in America. Cops stand at the end of the bridge,
see-through riot shields locked edge to edge.
Protecting us? protecting them? Lovers oblivious
clipping locks to locks, clicking cell phone photos
with the Mussolini eagles of the next bridge over
as backdrop. Lamps glowing the color of the moon.

"We don't like these," says Altadonna,
pointing at the protesters and maybe the police.
Sparrows roil great circles above us, half the time
going backwards while moving forward,
getting by almost not getting there,
brown backs wink in unison, white bellies flash
disappearing into their dive. Giuseppe shouts *"Suicidio!"*
and pretends to climb the bridge wall.
"Giuseppe!" Altadonna scolds. "Everytime
he sees Fascists he pretends he kills himself.
Rape and murder are not Gypsy crimes."
"Droghe," says Giuseppe. Altadonna: "Yes,
now they are into drugs. It changes everything.
I had a girlfriend, 30 years ago she spent three months
studying music with the Gypsies. She had no problems
living with them. Of course that was Hungary.
Of course it was Communists. Communists
knew how to make Gypsies happy.
Leave them alone."

First draft title: "On Listening for the First Time
to a €185,000 Ferrari Stopped by a Fascist Demonstration,"
couldn't make it work. One line worth saving:
"Backing out sounded like clearing the throat of god."

Giuseppe and Altadonna write their names on the biggest padlock
they can buy, size of a hand. *Argento titano.* They lock it,
throw the key in the river, now dusk purple.

9. *Batti Batti le Manine*

At the Caffé, Umberto the tweedy Sicilian travel agent
who came to Rome many years ago
loves to hold Maisie on his lap. We call him Umberto Umberto.
He teaches us a song: "Clap hands, daddy's coming,
he's bringing cookies and Maisie will eat them."
Settling down in his red plastic chair:
"I don't like to see any group targeted."
Stirring and sipping his *corretto.*
"On the other hand it looks bad to tourists,
these shit piles along the Tiber."

Tonight I sing
batti batti le manine, to Maisie,
my mosquito-bit, big-eyed baby,
we walk down the bank to the next bridge
che adesso vien papà
then back up the other bank, a half-mile, mile
che porta i biscottini
to get around a demonstration
e Maisie li mangerà

Something in the weather, a lightness. It's fall but feels like spring.
Rome rushes back, shapes itself around me.
"What do I have to be anxious about?" I say.
Singing, I pick Maisie out of her stroller.
My back aches.
Maisie leans and writhes.
At Ponte Milvio, the demonstration breaks up,
there's running, a stream of thug-boys
weaving through traffic
down the path to the Tiber bank

where human stink remains.
Face masks, bandanas pulled down—
one has a metal rod.

Here are the infinitives.
Spingere. To push (your teeth in where you want).
Dire. To say (nothing). *Interessarsi di.* To (not) care.
Avere. To have (a people who are the only ones who matter).
Restare impunito per.
To get away (with it when you need to get away).

10. *Rome and Its Night*

I want Blanca back.

Go away, we'll tell her, each time she gets near.

She'll steal from us if she gets a chance.

Why wouldn't she.

We'll have a bad feeling about the sway of her hips, her pushing mostly up
to men.

We'll tell her go away.

We can't tell her to go away.

The Gypsies are hounded out of Rome.

Sparrows level out, a net with the sparrows as knots.

Fifteen men run out of orangey streetlamp light at the Piazzale's edge.

Zingaro! Zingaro! Animale! down the river path.

Who they chase gets away because here they are coming back to the street.

They pull off their hoods and bandanas.

The crazy guy in the gold lamé vest with the shopping cart and the cross
around his neck shouts at the black crazy guy who drinks wine out of a
carton lying around on planters all day.

Maisie sleepily points at them. She likes to point.

There go Altadonna and Giuseppe—they got across.

Fascist boys going different directions now in groups of two and three.

One, I just noticed, alone.

Bandana down below his chin.

He has a puckered asshole for a mouth.

Holds his cosh loose by his side.

Batti batti le manine

He looks around at sparrow noise sucking itself down into a tree.

Restare impunito per.

He weighs the cosh. It's heavy.

He walks head down.

He thwacks at weeds.

Young, beautiful, frail as Blanca, he has a cross around his neck.

That has nothing to do with what I wanted to say.

On a Metro platform, a crazy woman banging her head against a pillar—
what do you do, just look away?
Bad things happening make you feel alive.
The moon high up is a Roman sight.
Umberto Umberto at the awning edge at the edge of night watches away from
the thugs into traffic, not wanting to have this in his life.
The last of the sparrows sweep into the tree in a panic of similes, a choral
cutoff, visual thump, like our twenty-first century, an afterbirth.
Rome and its night breathing
like a man on an oxygen tank
tubes shoved up his nose
opens and shuts his mouth, fishily,
rhythmically, trying for more air.

IV

Ask The Poetess: An Advice Column

DEAR POETESS—Who do you think was the greatest poetess of the twentieth century? Sara Teasdale? Or Adelaide Crapsey?—WONDERING

DEAR WONDERING—A usage note at dictionary.com states "many critics have argued that there are sexist connotations in the use of the suffix *–ess* to indicate a female in words like *sculptress, waitress, stewardess,* and *actress.* The heart of the problem lies in the nonparallel use of terms to designate men and women."

The Poetess has long felt that women's equality should be founded in the notion that a woman is *no worse than* a man. So it stands to reason that men are just as bad as women. The Poetess applies the term *poetess* to men and women, good poetesses and bad.

It's true that few poems surpass Ms. Adelaide Crapsey's subtly apostrophe'd lines from her cinquain "November Night," "Like steps of passing ghosts, / The leaves, frost-crisp'd, break from the trees / And fall." Or Ms. Sara Teasdale's "A November Night," "think that every path we ever took / Has marked our footprints in mysterious fire, / Delicate gold that only fairies see." What is a poetess without ghosts, fairies, mysteries—and other consolations? So, Mr. Charles Bukowski:

> *I was always a natural slob*
> *I liked to lay upon the bed*
> *in undershirt (stained, of*
> *course) (and with cigarette*
> *holes) shoes off*
> *beerbottle in hand*
> from "The Great Slob."

He is our greatest poetess.—LOVE THE POETESS

———

DEAR POETESS—I graduated from [Name of Famous Writing School deleted] in 1986. Ever since my doctor switched me from Prozac to Zoloft, I feel compelled to write poems attacking the linguistic hegemony of the bourgeois ruling class, sometimes using Google searches to generate strings of jargon and nonsense. Help! What should I do?—A STUDENT

DEAR POETESS—I graduated from [Name of Famous Writing School deleted] in 1999. Ever since my doctor switched me from Zoloft to Prozac, I feel tempted to write first-person poems about my childhood memories of my grandmother, a marvelous woman of ropey hands and gnarly wisdom. Help! What should I do?—A STUDENT

DEAR STUDENTS, CLASSSES OF '86 AND '99—Aren't you both missing hyphens from your signatures? Shouldn't that be A-Student? Did the Poetess Ezra Pound say, "Make it new enough so your teacher will give you an A?" He did not. Of course, the Poetess's heart goes out to you. (It's said the Poetess's heart goes rather indiscriminately out, but that is Just Unfair.) I advise you to go back to school and, this time around, flunk a couple of classes. If you can—it won't be easy—flunk out. It may change your life.—LOVE THE POETESS

―――――――

DEAR POETESS—I am a chemist. People at parties are always discovering this and saying to me, "A chemist? My favorite element is Iridium." This is driving me crazy.—OCUPATIONALLY HAZARDED

DEAR OH DEAR—It could be worse. Imagine if you had to hear "A poetess? My favorite poem is 'The Road Not Taken'" a hundred times a year.—LOVE THE POETESS

―――――――

DEAR POETESS—But seriously, what's the difference between a male poetess and a female poetess?—IT'S THE CHROMOSOMES, HUH?

DEAR ITCH—Okay, there is one difference. A male poetess can say "Gettin' soft, dude, gettin' soft!" while delivering a punch to another male poetess's expanding gut. A female poetess can never ever ever say this to her sisters in poetry, with punching or without.
—LOVE THE POETESS

DEAR POETESS—Now that I'm pregnant with my first child, friends and strangers put their hands on my belly and say things like "you're a poet, don't worry, having a baby is like writing a book." Is this even true?
—POET-MOM-TO-BE

DEAR POETESS—I love being a mom but my husband (we met when were both creative writing MFA students) complains I'm shortchanging myself and my talents because my attachment-parenting techniques—holding the children 24-7, co-sleeping, breastfeeding still going strong with Wystan, seven, Minaloy, four, and the twins Walt and Emily, two—have made some of our favorite adult activities impossible. He says "you never want to _____ anymore." He doesn't use the word "write" but I'm pretty sure that's what he means.
—MOTHER ADDICTED RELENTLESSLY TO YOUNG RASCALS

DEAR POETESS—Why do mothers think they're so special? Anybody can pop a child out. Writing a book of poems is much harder.—NULLIPARA

DEAR PO-MO, MARTYR AND NULL—Treat the poem as the child and the child as the poem. Failed babies should not be thrown away. Instead, tuck them in a drawer or save them on a memory stick—who knows when you'll want to dig them out, pull them apart and work them up again? Finished babies should be given classic or clever names, stamped *diagnostically-approved* by the Pediatric Industrial Complex Committee on Random Developmental Milestones, and multiply-submitted to kindergartens for publication. Meanwhile, poems should be burped, diapered and placed on their backs to sleep, however much they may scream and try to turn over. Corporal punishment is not recommended but if you must spank the poem, never do so in anger. The community remains divided on whether or not a daily vitamin is useful, but those Baby Tennyson Teach-Your-Poem-to-Rhyme-Before-It-Can-Scan and Baby Avant Teach-Your-Poem-to-Experiment-Before-It-Has-Even-Skimmed-*Paterson* DVDs have been thoroughly discredited and may be returned for store credit.

And remember, you can't finish a child or book without making lots of mistakes. Confidential to Mr. Martyr: Nagging will get you nowhere, in bed or out. Try champagne, oysters and mopping the damn floor for a change.—LOVE THE POETESS

DEAR POETESS—I've been asked by my favorite cousin to read a poem at her wedding. Do you have any suggestions?—UNPOETICAL

DEAR UNPO—Resist the temptation, no matter how many flutes of headache-inducing cheap sugary California champagne you've had, to read all twenty-three stanzas of Spenser's "Epithalamion" out of spite. Try, instead, rejiggering clichés of wedding poetry such as Thomas Hardy's "In Time of 'The Breaking of Nations.'" Of course, your cousin, in this day and age, is likely no "maid" in the strict sense of the word; then again, your cousin-in-law is likely no "wight"; you and your extended family have probably never been seen "harrowing clods" and no one really knows for sure what "couch grass" is. Still, the message, with a little tinkering, remains:

> *Yet this will go onward the same*
> *Though (Bush) Dynasties pass*

and

> *(Undeclared) War's annals (however incomplete as written and*
> *televised by the self-censoring sheeplike U.S. press corps)*
> *will cloud into night*
> *Ere their story die.*

—LOVE THE POETESS

DEAR POETESS—I'm bored. I know, we must not say so. But as a fact I'm bored with life, bored with poetry, bored even with Sudoku. I'm beginning to think that life, friends, is boring. What should I do?—NOTHING NEW UNDER THE SUN

DEAR NONUTS—Hmm. You sound heavy bored. The Poetess e.e. cummings once said to me when he was feeling blue (perhaps in the sense of blue movies?), "Girlboys may nothing more than boygirls need." I said to e.e., "e.e. dear, you should write that down," and do you know, he did?—LOVE THE POETESS

DEAR POETESS—*Do you think dirty words belong in poetry?*—SOAP-IN-MOUTH POET

DEAR POETESS—*I don't think politics has any place in poetry. Am I right?*—GET OVER POLITICS

DEAR SIMP AND GOP—The Authoress Stendhal wrote, "Poetry in wartime is like a violin played on a pistol range. The sound does not harmonize with any other instrument."* I feel that dirty thoughts are fine, as are political thoughts, but that the *words* should be cleaned up with dashes, as I have done for this stanza (excessively frank in its language on both counts) by a famous old poetess unknown to me:

> *A------, A------,*
> *G-d sh-- his ----- on thee*
> *And crown thy good*
> *with b------hood*
> *from --- to shining ---.*

This is not censorship. Everyone will know what you mean.
—LOVE THE POETESS

DEAR POETESS—*Why do people write confessional poetry when they can just go to church and make confession?*—P. BENEDICT SEDICESIMO

* A friend says Stendhal wrote "Politics in literature is like a pistol fired at a concert"—but not in my translation.

DEAR BEN—In church confession, Catholics confess their sins. In confessional poetry persons of all faiths confess how others have sinned against them.—LOVE THE POETESS

———————

DEAR POETESS—Thank you for your response to my last question. Can you help me with a new trouble? My wife keeps messing with the magnetic loops I put on the back of my Ford Excursion. She crosses out the Tr *so that instead of "Support Our Troops" they read "Support Our Oops." I get upset but she says it's Flarf. Do you agree?—A-STUDENT '86 (I took your advice about that hyphen.)*

DEAR A-STUDENT—Just because everyone doesn't know what Flarf is, doesn't mean everyone doesn't know what Flarf isn't.
—LOVE THE POETESS

———————

DEAR POETESS—What is poetry and if you know what poetry is what is prose?—GERTRUDE

DEAR GERTRUDE—Exactly. Love to you & Alice.—THE POETESS

———————

DEAR POETESS—As you can see in my signature below, I took your advice about that hyphen. But otherwise you weren't very helpful. Why can't *I write poems about my grandma? She was a wonderful woman!—A-STUDENT '99*

DEAR A-STUDENT—Exactly.—LOVE THE POETESS

———————

DEAR POETESS—My poetry teacher keeps saying things like "Poetry is what you get when your language aspires to be more than utilitarian. Install power

words to produce jolts of feeling." Recently I noticed he does this with his eyes closed. Who should I report this to?—21ˢᵗ CENTURY POET

DEAR 21ˢᵗ CENTURY POET—Is your teacher an adjunct with a double-full-time teaching load at $2,500 per class, without health insurance, job security or other benefits? Overworked teachers generally have a talent for teaching while sleeping. I'm surprised you noticed. In my day students universally practiced their own version: listening while sleeping.—LOVE THE POETESS

DEAR POETESS—I am truly grateful for the work you are doing to bring the term poetess *back into acceptability. There is a women's poetry, don't you agree? After all, women are more emotional than men, especially in their poems.—DIFFERENCE FEMINIST*

DEAR DIFF—Oh, I do, I do agree. Especially when one compares poems like, say, Poetess Marianne Moore's "The Fish" with Poetess Alfred Lord Tennyson's "Tears, Idle Tears."—LOVE THE POETESS

DEAR POETESS—Speaking of Moore, I finally got around to checking out Garrison Keillor's Good Poems *anthology. In his intro, he writes, "Marianne Moore was a dotty old aunt whose poems are quite replicable for anyone with a thesaurus. A nice lady, but definitely a plodder."—APPALLED*

DEAR APPALLED—The Poetess admires Garrison Keillor's politics, taste in music, and especially Dusty, Lefty and Guy Noir (she even found inspiration for a poem of her own in one of his charming characters). And let's not forget the annual joke show! The Poetess refuses to criticize the taste in poetry of those who delight her—even when they seem to be reveling in creeping yahooism at its creepiest. —LOVE THE POETESS

DEAR POETESS—How can we get more readers for poetry?
—OUTREACHER

DEAR OUTREACHER—Can you explain what you mean by
"we"?—LOVE THE POETESS

DEAR POETESS—I mean those of us, like you and me, who understand
that this wounded world badly needs poetry's spiritual wisdoms. That is, how
can we reach out to those who enjoy rap, poetry slams and cowboy poetry?—
OUTREACHER

DEAR OUTREACHER—When I'm not quite sure what to say—and
I think it is important for my readers to understand that I too am
occasionally uncertain—I trust to the wisdom of chance operations,
close my eyes and put my finger down anywhere in the nearest book.
I did this for your question. As the Poetess Frank O'Hara says in
"Memorial Day 1950," "I hear the sewage singing / underneath my
bright white toilet seat and know / that somewhere sometime it will
reach the sea."—LOVE THE POETESS

———

DEAR POETESS—It's obvious you make up all your questions. What's
the funniest answer you have for which you haven't been able to make up a
question?—O. LI PO

DEAR MR. LI PO—F=R=A=N=G=L=A=I=S.
—LOVE THE POETESS

———

Note: The Poetess has received dozens of questions about a certain
William Carlos Williams poem. She will answer a representative
selection.

I think that wet red wheelbarrow is actually womb imagery, affirming the feminine principal and women's fertility. Don't you agree?—WOMYN OF MANY BLESSINGS

I was walking around today after class going "So much depends . . . but what, what depends?" Then I thought, maybe it's "depends" in the sense of "hang down," as in "And ever-living Lamps depend in Rows" from Alexander Pope's "The Temple of Fame." Is the Williams poem an homage to eighteenth-century wit?—ONLY BEING SENSIBLE, CREATIVE, USEFUL, REAL AND ELEGANT

Am I right to consider "The Red Wheelbarrow" a snide joke on the poetry-reading populace?—TESTY TRADITIONAL WORDSMITH IN TULSA

I feel that Williams is standing beside that wheelbarrow, just outside the frame, smiling at us and saying, "come along with me, everything will be okay." Do you think this is a good interpretation?—HOPEFUL, EVEN AFTER LIFE IS NO GOOD

I think "The Red Wheelbarrow" would be a better poem if it incorporated meter and rhyme, don't you?—NEVER ENOUGH ORGANIZATIONAL CRITERIA OR NIGGLING

If I sat my grandmother in a red wheelbarrow, then *could I write poems about her?*—A-STUDENT '99

DEAR WOMB, OBSCURE, TESTY TWIT, HEALING, NEOCON AND A-STUDENT—My answers to you, in order are: no, no, no, no, no and yes!—LOVE THE POETESS

———

If you would like to Ask The Poetess a question, write to her at askthepoetess@ hotmail.com.

NOTES

In "A Snow Woman," the last line is from Paul Valéry's "Le cimitière marin": *a long look on the calm of gods.*

In "This Need Not Be a Comment on Death," the Camille Paglia quote is from *Break, Blow, Burn: Camille Paglia Reads Forty-three of the World's Best Poems.*

In "Ippopotamo," La Specola, where the poem's stuffed hippo is found, is a science museum in Florence, Italy, where hundreds of taxidermy animals are lined up in cases in room after room. *Assisted readymade* is Marcel Duchamp's term for the ordinary objects he selected, modified and exhibited. Most of this poem is a lineated version of an anonymous English translation of the explanatory card accompanying the hippo.

In "Elegy," the Scrovegni Chapel is where Giotto painted his fresco cycle of the lives of the Virgin Mary and of Jesus.

In "Attenti agli Zingari," Italian not translated immediately in the body of the poem translates as follows: in section 1, *Odori, Ospitalità*: chopped vegetable soup base, hospitality; *minestra*: soup; *animali . . . nessuna ospitalità a questi animali*: animals . . . no hospitality for these animals; in section 3, *FUMO UCCIDE*: smoking kills; *Rita-Gianni sempre*: Rita-Gianni forever; *USA merda . . . Napoli merda*: USA shit . . . Naples shit; in section 9, *corretto*: espresso "corrected" with a shot of booze.

ACKNOWLEDGMENTS

Thanks to the editors of the following journals for first publishing the poems and advice in this manuscript, sometimes in different form: *American Poetry Review*: "Attenti Agli Zingari," "Lyric," "This Need Not Be a Comment on Death"; *filling Station*: "Thrash"; *Literary Imagination*: "L'Allegro: Driving Home"; *London Review of Books*: "Her Failed Band, 1982," "His Failed Band, 1973," "The Spirit Award"; *Massachusetts Review*: "Perpetual Youth Lost by Humankind"; *Nation*: "Women's Poetry"; *New Republic*: "Midnight Feeding"; *Ploughshares*: "Kissinger at the Louvre (Three Drafts)"; *Plume*: "A Snow Woman"; *Poetry*: "Ask the Poetess," "Econo Motel, Ocean City," "Elegy," "Il Penseroso: The Fat Lady," "Torment"; *Poetry Northwest*: "Inside All This"; *Threepenny Review*: "Ippopotamo," "Metaphor for Something, or Solving the Credit Crunch," "Stolen Vehicle Discovered at the Junkyard"; *Valparaiso Poetry Review*: "Liberalism."

The *Manchester Review* (UK) republished and published for the first time online "Il Penseroso: The Fat Lady," "Kissinger at the Louvre (Three Drafts)," and "Thrash."

Thanks to the Guggenheim Foundation, the Pennsylvania Council on the Arts and Smith College for their support during the writing of these poems.